Charting Your Life's Roadmap

in an Uncertain World

Choose Happiness Daily

NUALA DUIGNAN

Copyright © Nuala Duignan, 2013

The author has asserted her moral rights

First Published in 2013 by The Manuscript Publisher,
publishing solutions for the digital age -www.TheManuscriptPublisher.com

ISBN: 978-0-9571157-7-4

A CIP Catalogue record for this book is available from the British Library

Typesetting, page layout and cover design by DocumentsandManuscripts.com

Cover illustrations by Colm Holmes and Oscar Duggan

Printed and bound in Ireland

Contents   Page

Foreword

About Coaching

Coaching originated in United Sates in 1980's as a result of the realisation of therapists that many of their clients did not require therapy as such, rather, more professional support towards directing their future path. Also, it was noted the great success sports coaching was having in the United States.

Coaching has become one of the fastest growing businesses in the world today. As well as private individuals, companies are discovering the positive benefits of their employees availing of coaching support. The process encourages you to take ownership of your life and help you focus on your strengths and become more self-aware. Coaching helps you to discover your real passion and find out what you love in life.

Why delay the process of moving on?

If you feel you can do with some assistance in exploring those positives in your life, remember that help is never far away. Life Coaching will assist and support you in becoming more aware of the positive influences in your surroundings. Don't delay the process of change.

This book contains many questions for you to answer, offering you unexpected insights about yourself. Developing new habits and actively building on the positives in your life are my aims in this publication.

As a Professional Life and Business Coach, over recent years, I have seen many people improve the quality of their lives. I have assisted my clients to help themselves towards more satisfied living. The people whom I have helped have ranged across all ages, income brackets and industries. Working with individuals towards the results they crave has little to do with my expertise, but rather **their determination to find their own answers**. This is because we each have an inbuilt *roadmap* for our own lives. This *roadmap* describes the life we are meant to live, the life that will bring us the most happiness and satisfaction with least effort.

As a Life Coach, I find it exceptionally rewarding to work with people towards reaching their full potential. It is very fulfilling to observe their surprise as they achieve more than they ever thought possible, sometimes even discovering new strengths they were previously unaware of.

Integrity, trust and a genuine belief in the individual are central to my coaching practice, coupled with a focused approach and a belief in the possibilities for each person. For me now, care, concern and focus on my clients and where they want to reach, is my driving force. I help them decide which goal they truly want but more importantly, support them on their journey towards reaching their goal. I feel passionate about the benefits of Life Coaching. In this book I include Testimonials from some of my clients.

"We should not fear opening ourselves up to places that scare us. When we touch those places the light gets in."
– Tony Bates

PART 1
Life Coaching

1.1   What Is Life Coaching?

Coaching is about *waking up* to what is possible for you. It's about bridging that *gap* from where you are to where you want to reach.

Life Coaching is a one-to-one interactive relationship based upon confidentiality, respect and trust, where the Coach is a skilled listener. As a Life Coach I do not give advice, instead I encourage and challenge my client to find his/her own solutions. Your coach will hear all that is said but more importantly he/she will hear that which is unsaid.

Life Coaching is a means of exploring choices and gaining new perspectives in a safe environment.

The reasons for life coaching are the ones bouncing around in your head at this very moment. The question now is:

Are you ready for the rewards that come with taking your game of life to the next level?

1.2   Benefits of Life Coaching

Life Coaching offers you that time, space and encouragement to focus on you, and what you would like to achieve. This process facilitates the possibility of real change in your life. Coaching is about helping you help yourself.

Your Life Coach prompts you to focus on real issues you may be having. You will get that gentle yet firm *push* towards working on your desired results. You will be working towards a point where your life *clicks*. Your Coach will not provide you with the answers, as only you know what changes you need to make. Coaching will encourage you to figure things out for yourself, with a view to leaving the past behind and moving towards a more fulfilled future.

What is important to remember is that **you set the agenda**, not the Coach. This is about **Your Life**.

Are there aspects of your life about which you feel you have no choice?

Do you know what is really important to you?

Do you find yourself looking over your shoulder at the negative things that happened to you in the past?

Is your happiness something that is going to happen when you achieve this or that or when you retire?

Do you worry a lot about tomorrow, next week or next year?

Testimonial 1

Nuala coached me around the establishment of my own business over a period of three months.

Nuala is no ordinary Life Coach. She is a person with passion, relentless drive and energy for doing the best for her clients. Her own vast experience, knowledge and understanding of life inspire and encourage her clients. She has a very unique and personal approach to her work.

Most of all, is her amazing ability to seek out the best in the people she works with, directing them and driving them towards their goals.

Having worked with Nuala as my Professional Business Advisor and Personal Life Coach, I would highly recommend her to anybody who feels they could benefit from support or direction in their personal or business life.

Marie, Film Producer, Co. Leitrim

Testimonial 2

As an engineer I assumed that going to a life coach I could present a set of problems, reveal my qualifications and through using something like a mathematical formula, I would be provided with a set of answers and job titles which may suit me! However, on leaving the sessions with Nuala, I understood that Life Coaching is much more expansive than that. It is a partnership whereby the client decides the agenda, and the coach encourages forward movement towards the client's goal.

Thanks to the support and encouragement from Nuala, I have the confidence now to explore my interests/hobbies and I am now seeing an avenue whereby my hobby can become a source of income.

From Ray, Engineer, Dundrum Town Centre.

PART 2

Goals and Outcomes

2.1   Goals Make Your Life Self-Directed

You cannot get what you want until you describe what it is you want. What do you see yourself doing if there were no perceived obstacles in your way? Give yourself the freedom to explore your options and the answers you are seeking will appear.

What is it you want?

Why do you want it?

By what date do you want it?

What actions do you need to take to get there?

What is your first action?

Begin by choosing a goal that's important to you.

Write it down.

Now figure out what you can **reasonably achieve** within six months.

Write that action down.

WHY do you want this goal?

WHAT in yourself or externally, would prevent you from achieving it?

Think about a previous achievement you've had, be it big or small.

WHAT motivated you then to pursue that goal?

What kept you going?

What's the one action you need to take to get started on your current goal?

This will probably be a small action because it's just getting you started.

When will you take this action?

It takes time to get through this exercise but if it pushes you to achieve just one of your goals, it's worth it.

If you're going to try this, do it **now** before you decide to put it off for another day.

Remember the words of Edward Young

> *"Procrastination is the thief of time."*

Now, imagine you have already achieved that goal. Write down the answers to the following questions:

How do you feel about yourself and your world?

How do other people respond to you?

What is your day like?

2.2 You Accomplish More with an Outcome Focus

Set Yourself Realistic Goals using the acronym: SMART

Specific

Measurable

Achievable

Realistic

Timely

One of the distinct gifts of being human is our ability to create our own destiny. Isn't it surprising then how many of us never accept this gift or just give it away, making somebody else responsible for it?

Here's the bottom line. The future is coming and there's nothing you can do to stop it. Your goals may take some work. Worthy goals usually do. You can choose to take action now, accomplish those goals and enjoy the rewards, or you can still be putting them off five years from now. Let us begin to understand that the only thing preventing us from reaching our goals is ourselves. When we continue to do as we've always done, we will continue to get the same results.

You get to decide, right now, where you want to reach. Dream those possibilities. Set the intention. If you could have it any way you wanted, what would it be? What would it feel like?

> *"Most of us seem to spend our lives as if we have another one in the bank."*
> – **B. Irwin**

2.3   Don't allow Change Distract you from your Goals.

The idea of change is not new. The most common response to change is resistance. We resist change because of our fear of the unknown and our desire to remain in our "comfort zone". Often we look back with nostalgia and see the past as a brighter time. People who fear change often see themselves as victims. They feel unprepared to conquer whatever may come.

Set daily, weekly and monthly goals to keep the momentum going. Persistence and forward movement is what will help you reach your goal. Remember why you started on this path that you have chosen for yourself. Once you're moving in the direction of your goals you will enjoy '*the journey*'. Enjoy your daily progress and celebrate your areas of accomplishment. If you do not have fun with the steps you take forward, what is the point in continuing? Congratulate yourself on discovering that you can handle anything that comes your way.

By setting goals and working towards achieving them you will grow into a happier you. Now is the time to think anew, clarify situations, discard waste and encourage new growth.

> *"Life is not a Rehearsal, It's a Performance."*
> – **Michael Caine**

> *"What we do today, right now, will have an accumulated effect on all our tomorrows."*
> – **A. Stoddard**

2.4   The Wheel of Life is a powerful tool which opens

up a new world for the client. He/she can see which areas of their lives are working and which are not. It helps you to quickly identify the areas to which you need to bring more balance and the areas to which you want to devote more time and energy. It also helps you understand where you might want to cut back. The challenge is to use this knowledge and work towards a more balanced life. The Wheel of Life is a powerful tool because it gives you a clear vision of your current way of life, compared with the way you'd ideally like it to be. It is called the Wheel of Life because each area of your life is mapped on a circle, like the spokes of a wheel.

When life is busy, or all your energy is focused in a particular direction, it's all too easy to find yourself *off balance*, not paying enough attention to important areas. That's when it's time to take a review of your life, so that you can bring things back into balance. It will become apparent that no one area of your life is Your Identity, e.g. you are not identified by your employment or lack of employment as the case may be. It is only one-eighth of your overall Wheel of Life.

The eight sections of the wheel represent balance. Regarding the centre of the wheel as zero and the outer edge as ten, rank your level of satisfaction with each area you have chosen as relevant to your current life. Rank each area by drawing a line to create a new outer edge, see example below. When you have scored all areas join the points on each section to draw a wheel. This will show you how balanced your overall life is going and the areas you really need to focus on and set goals for improvement. The new perimeter of the circle represents your current Wheel of Life. From there you choose the area you need to begin working on and begin setting goals to improve those key areas. (*Review Goal Setting in previous chapter 2.1.*)

Explanation of each section as follows:

1.   Your Finance

This is not so much about what you have but rather about your level of satisfaction or otherwise with what you have in relation to your finances. There are some millionaires who constantly worry about their finances and concern themselves with the accumulation of more so they would score very low here. On the other hand, people who have just enough to get by but are contented human beings and accept their situation as it is. They will score high on the Wheel of Life.

2.   Personal Development

People who commit themselves to learning and improving themselves can give themselves a high rating on the Wheel. Individuals, who are committed to learning as much as possible about their life and enjoy experiencing new opportunities. Being open to improving and *stretching* themselves. The fact that you are reading this book demonstrates a certain level of commitment to Personal Development!.

3.   Your Health

We all take our health for granted until it lets us down.

How is yours?

Do you look after yourself?

Are you eating well?

Do you take regular exercise?

Having a poor level of health does not mean you give you yourself a low score, the scoring depends on how you handle your poor health. A person may have full health and yet have a negative outlook and be miserable in life. Very often people who have been dealt poor health are an inspiration to the rest of us as they handle their situation in a positive manner.

4.   Family and Friends

This section will affect other areas of your life. In this respect family and friends mean different things to different people depending on their current situation. Marking your level of contentment on the Wheel depends on how happy or otherwise you are with your family life and friends. Whatever family life means to you give yourself a current score.

5.   Fun and Recreation

Are you having enough fun and recreation in your life? If you are dissatisfied with the level of recreation and fun you are having, mark this section accordingly. Then decide what actions you will need to put in place to increase the fun element of your life. For example, you may have to decide to factor more time in your week to do whatever it is you enjoy most, be it exercise, reading a good book or enjoying an evening out.

6.   Outlook and Attitude

Attitude is vital and will influence every aspect of your life.

Is your glass half full or half empty?

Are you a positive person who notices all the good things in your life?

Are you that person who comes up with action steps towards solutions when things do not go as planned? Or do you always expect the worst outcome?

7.   Career

How is your career going? Do you feel sick before you go to work each morning or do you go into work with a smile on your face? If you are not working, do you know what it is you would love to do but never had a chance previously? Are you putting steps in place towards developing the work you would love to do. (*See Paragraph 6.2*). Rank yourself according to your level of current contentment with your work or your level of success with the steps you are taking towards future employment.

8.   Your Environment

Our surroundings influence our outlook and mood hugely. Because of this it is essential that your work space inspires you and going home feels likes a sanctuary. On challenging days your home should act as an escape from the outside world. As much as possible try and have your home reflect your personality. In this section rate your level of satisfaction with the lay-out and décor of your home. You can choose to focus on your work space either. Following on from this exercise it should become clear to you what small steps you can put in place to improve your Environment.

Now that you have a picture of your **current life balance** and your **ideal life balance**. What are the gaps? These are the areas of your life that need attention. Once you have completed the wheel put a date on it and then review it at least every six months. Hopefully you will have made significant progress in the areas that you decided to work and focus on. Three or six months later there will always be another area that will require your focus.

The Wheel of Life

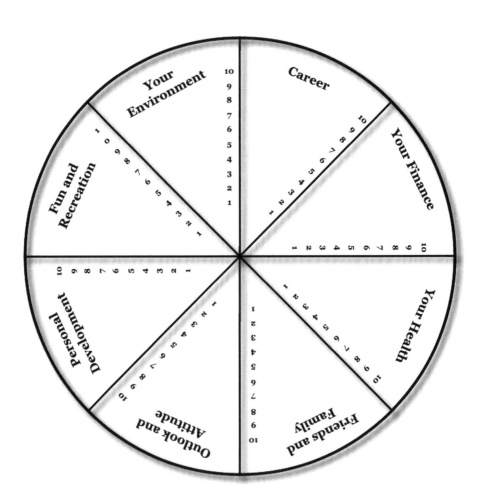

Example

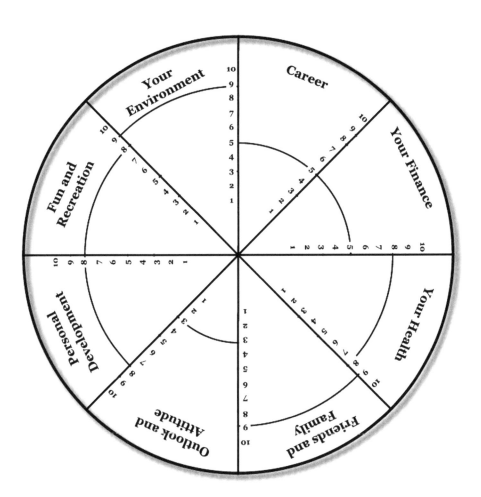

Testimonial 1

Before I started my coaching journey, I was at a place in my life where I was stuck; I just did not know how to get going again.

I had read some of Nuala's articles in my local paper The Liffey Champion, *and decided to make contact.*

We met, and Nuala explained the Wheel of Life and how to rate each segment in it. The result was like a light bulb being switched on in my head.

With the eight sections of the wheel representing balance, Nuala showed me some simple techniques in ranking my level of satisfaction within the various areas in my life. I then began to work on the relevant segments, always aiming towards a 10. When the initial sections were worked on, I then moved on to the next relevant section of my life which required some work. Nuala emphasised to me the importance of viewing the Wheel of Life (in other words my overall life) on a regular basis and acknowledge myself on my daily progress. I would never have previously considered acknowledging myself and viewing the positivities in my life.

Many thanks Nuala for the guided journey!

John, Business Owner, Dublin South.

Testimonial 2

*At our first meeting, I immediately felt relaxed and at ease in Nuala's company. Any problems I had felt were impossible, Nuala soon made me realise you can overcome your challenges and achieve your **goals**. Her approach was simple and straight forward: "Break your goals down into baby steps, allowing time for relaxation," and she reinforced the importance of exercise and a healthy diet as a natural de-stressor.*

Nuala helped to restore my confidence and self-belief. If you really want to do something in your life, you can. Positivity, a good attitude and a realistic planning process is all you need.

Carol, Co. Leitrim

PART 3

Your Attitude to the World

3.1 If Attitudes were for Sale, Would You Buy Yours?

Unless we learn to change our attitude and begin to overcome some of the psychological blocks which keep holding us back from doing what we would like, we will remain where we are at. There are seven main psychological blocks which can hold us back and prevent us from moving forward in our lives:

Blame– Blaming others or circumstances beyond your control. Try beating blame as it stops you taking responsibility for your life and it convinces you that you are powerless.

Risk Taking– By never taking a risk, life can become '*flat*' and very little happens. Unfortunately, anxiety and fear often holds us back, so this must be dealt with.

Don't Judge– Try not to judge yourself or others. If you judge, you can get yourself annoyed and irritated by events and situations which you cannot change and in the process you overlook all the positivity in your life.

Indecision – Let go of indecision as you will "*back away*" from key situations just because you're not sure of the outcome. Major causes of indecision can stem from previous disappointments. It is better to experience a degree of failure than never to have tried at all.

Procrastination – By putting off until tomorrow you forfeit your ability to overcome challenges. Procrastination occurs when courage is weak. Give up worrying about not "*being ready*". Just do whatever it is you fear.

Forget trying to be Perfect– When nothing is good enough you will be unable to enjoy what you have, or who you are. Although perfectionists are often most accomplished in their '*field*', they are rarely good enough for themselves. Rather than love what they have created, perfectionists are seldom happy with their own work.

Abandon Self-Pity – When focusing on your blessings you are moving the focus from what is missing in your life to

25

all of that is right. Feeling sorry for yourself prevents you from recognising new opportunities.

The greatest security comes when you trust yourself enough not to be phased by what's to come. Instead, throw yourself into your life/your work and apply your skills.

> *"Do that which is within you. Take no heed of gestures which would beckon you aside."*
> **- Frederick Dey**

3.2   An Attitude of Gratitude

We all have a basic level of happiness, a range of joy we'll stay within regardless of our external circumstances. The greatest factor in determining the level of this joy is our mental attitude. Instead of feeling we must change our circumstances, we should try changing the way we interpret those circumstances. It sounds easier said than done because if we've always seen the *glass half-empty*, it will be unlikely that we will transform into a positive thinker overnight. We cannot always control what happens to us but **we do have the power to control how we respond**, which ultimately indicates how we feel.

> *"Many of us spend half our time wishing for things that we could have if we didn't spend half our time wishing."*
> **- Alexander Woolcott**

Having an attitude of gratitude will enable you to realise all that's good and right in your life before you begin to confront a difficult situation. Always review the positives in your life. There are three categories of people:

Those who say it can't happen

Those who make it happen and

Those who ask, "*What happened?*"

Success in these times can be classed as going from failure to failure without a loss of enthusiasm. So, get motivated today, take action and build your own moment in life.

"Do what you can, with what you have, wherever you are."
– Theodore Roosevelt

Gratitude is all about appreciating the things we have in our lives. It is a way of reaching back to our natural state of happiness. We get to notice what's right instead of what's wrong.

Cultivate an *'attitude of gratitude'* by being mindful daily of all we have. Because we are so *'hardwired'* to pay attention to the negatives we forget to pay attention to all the positives in our lives.

We can begin to think of the things in our lives which we usually take for granted, particularly our good health. Add all the things that we cannot survive without, such as fresh air, water and food. In times of challenge why not consider some of the above.

Appreciate the weather too, whatever it may bring. After all, it is the rainwater that sustains the natural beauty around us. Stop and listen to the bird song and smell the roses.

We can do something for somebody for no reason other than simply wanting to do it. Have no attachment to the outcome. It does not always have to be a grand gesture just to have an impact on somebody. It can be the simple things that count. Often it's a smile, a look or a gesture that helps to connect. Post a card to somebody with whom you have not been in touch for a while. Most mail nowadays is junk mail or bills, so why not brighten somebody's day?

Count your blessings and be thankful. Create a trail of happiness as you go forward in your life.

"If you want to lift yourself up, lift someone else up first."
– Booker T. Washington

3.3   That Inner Smile

A smile is something money can't buy. **Positive attitude** comes with a smile! It is very easy to slip into negative thinking. Optimists have failures too, but they tend to regard these failures as temporary and specific to this instance. For the negative person however, they claim it is their own fault and it always happens to them. They take Murphy's Law to heart, '*if it can go wrong, it will.*' A smile releases endorphins which give you a natural high. Whilst reading this, recall a great positive and enjoyable experience in your life.

Feel that inner smile.

Much of our mood comes down to feeling in control of what happens in our life. This determines how we deal with the unpleasant happenings that befall all of us at some time. With a positive attitude we:

1.   Identify the stressor

2.   Take a problem-solving approach

3.   Deal with it as best you can.

One temptation that besets many of us is to take ourselves too serious and adopt an attitude of what can be called *learnt helplessness*. We can attach *too much weight* to unimportant incidents in our lives. Humour is a wonderful tool for *shaping us back down to size.* So let's be grateful for the gift of true humour, wherever we encounter it. It gives us strength to continue on. Laughter does not mean carelessness. Each of us must make our way through these serious times, carefully ordering our priorities and doing what we need to do to survive.

We can make of our experiences what we choose. We can focus on the traffic snarls while on our journey or we can smile at the thought that we are able to drive to our destination. Every experience offers us an opportunity to respond. That response is usually a reflection of our emotions. We choose to be angry or afraid. We can just as easily decide to be happy or confident. Even though we have got mad for years over traffic jams, it does not mean we can't give up the anger. How liberating it will be to claim back control of our positive emotions and our attitudes. You can decide to allow your thoughts control you, or you control them and put them to work positively for you. Censor your thoughts and banish the negative ones. It takes effort, but it can be done. You don't have to go around with a foolish grin on your face – but do experiment with that inner smile, it works wonders!

3.4   Your Attitude is your Window to the World

Everybody gets stuck at some point. It's how we get out of it that counts.

Your attitude is something that is within your control. When you leave home each day, the attitude with which you leave is for you to choose. Go out into the world with a good attitude and it's like having a crystal clear windscreen in your car, you can see things clearly.

Sometimes, more than any other factor, your attitude will determine what you will accomplish in the course of your day. Choose your attitude and don't let others, or current circumstances determine it for you.

In reality, there is a lot of fear around these times, around work or the lack of it, mounting bills or the fear of repossession of our homes. It's difficult not to personalise redundancy, but it is important to remember that it is not you, but rather that job that has become redundant. Immediately following on from redundancy, we need to see what we can salvage.

We can very easily be tempted to think negatively at times like these and say things like, 'I can't, I won't or I should not change', whilst others see it as a new opportunity. What can you do that others cannot do? When you have a more positive attitude there is no room for that negative thinking. Instead, you will feel much better both physically and mentally and you will also find yourself taking more positive actions. On the flip side, when you are negative in your thinking, you will find yourself taking less action.

All the "bad stuff" happening in the world today can make you feel down. We must bear in mind though, that all this negative news can get over-emphasised by the media. Fear can act as a means of persuasion. Are you allowing the media to persuade you into a doom and gloom mindset?

Why not take the next month and actively decide to avoid much of the negative news you see on TV and read in the newspapers. It is often this bad news that consumes your thoughts and doesn't allow the positive thoughts a chance. By eliminating the negatives you will naturally become a more positive person. This comes from what you read, what you listen to, and the people you spend your time with.

3.5   Moving from Negative to Positive Thoughts

Exercise changes your brain chemistry and induces natural happy hormones (endorphins) from the inside, so you feel better. Exercise has also been proven to help those suffering from mild depression. Be careful however when taking that walk or whatever form of exercise not to take your troubles or negative thoughts with you. Your thoughts rule your life, so let them be positive. Negative thinking has a corrosive effect on you, and you become hard on yourself. If you are angry about something, remember the anger is down to you. No one injects you with it. Things happen to thousands of people, but you can choose how you rationalise things for yourself.

> "A man is but the product of his thoughts. What he thinks, he becomes."
> – **Mahatma Gandhi**

Sometimes we are our own worst enemies when it comes to our thoughts. If somebody has a defeatist attitude such as: 'nothing will work' or 'there is no point talking to anyone', they will remain stuck and not 'let the light in'.

Testimonial 1

Having read one of Nuala's articles in the Offaly Independent, *I was hoping to get a better view of my next career move.*

*I met with Nuala, who made me feel completely at ease. A key question for me, which Nuala raised, was **"what will suffer if you don't make the necessary changes?"** This was a thought provoking question for me and immediately shifted my mindset. It was clear that things had already begun to suffer, my health and personal relationships. Whilst I knew this was happening, I had never previously asked myself that question.*

My short time with Nuala, gave me a clear perspective on my current situation.

Many thanks Nuala for that re-awakening which I needed and as a result I am now on my way to new living, in both my personal and work life.

Sandra, Offaly.

Testimonial 2

Hi Nuala,

I found your course to be of great benefit. What I most liked was the gathering of a group of people with a positive outlook, who wanted more for themselves and for their lives, and that hopefulness and striving for more rubbed off on me. My own thinking about my future and the possibilities and opportunities available to me are now subtly altered.

I have had my work hours reduced and was uncertain about what to do next and discovered your course quite by chance when enrolments were taking place in the Swan Centre in Rathmines. It seemed interesting and a way to get myself back into a college environment. Six months later I have just begun a full-time course in Design in Multimedia (while continuing to work part time) and I have signed up for evening classes in figure drawing and painting, something I was good at many years ago! I am now also a regular visitor to the gym where I am preparing to take part in a 10km run in the New Year. So I have come a long way from the beginning of the year when I was unsure of where I would end up. Now I have decided for myself that by next summer I will have the skills to create my own website (as I have a body of work to display there). Concrete, achievable goals, you might say! Many thanks for the great guidance and training Nuala.

Gerard, Rathmines

PART 4

Self-Confidence

4.1   How To Build Self-Esteem

How we see ourselves is more important than how anyone else sees us.

If we don't work at accepting ourselves, nothing anyone else thinks will matter.

Boosting That Self-Esteem

There is no one else like you on this planet. No one looks like you, has the same talents, experiences or perspective as you do. You are unique and you are here to make your unique contribution. If we each focus on what we bring into the world to share, there can be no comparisons, envy or regret. We are all here to '*contribute a verse*'.

Give it your best. When you do the best you can, with the best of what you've got, you can't help but feel good about yourself, and that confidence will shine through in everything you do.

Persevere. Everybody has setbacks and obstacles to contend with. Don't let them undermine your confidence. Treat them as opportunities to strengthen your resolve and then persevere.

Overcome Adversity. Overcoming adversity builds and strengthens self-confidence. The greatest songs, works of art and literary pieces have been written by people who have experienced the depths of despair, loss and emptiness and overcame them. Experiencing sadness and loss and then rising above it gives rise to hope and triumph. It makes you *stretch* and become more than you were before.

Accomplish Something. Set goals for yourself and then push yourself to reach them. Self-confidence soars when you succeed at what you put your mind to. It makes you feel unstoppable.

Separate yourself from the Event. You are not what happens to you or how you believe others see you. **You are who you choose to be** – a person of character, dignity and self-confidence.

Confront your Fears. There's nothing that destroys self-confidence more than succumbing to fear. Everybody feels fear at various times, we are all human. However, facing circumstances with courage and poise strengthens our character and builds our self-confidence. Fear can be described as below:

False

Evidence

Appears

Real

4.2   Give yourself a *Pep Talk*.

We all have our down moments, moments of doubt, confusion and uncertainty. When this happens we have to learn how to restore our self-esteem. One way of doing this is to understand that everybody goes through such moments. The thing to do is to recall all your past achievements and successes. Visualise your desired outcome and work towards that outcome. Practice makes perfect!

We can indeed feel helpless, negative and lethargic, sometimes, even frustrated and resentful by the situations we find ourselves in. We can live in fear which is determined by circumstances we perceive as beyond our control. The opposite of powerlessness however, is being in control, an ability to tackle the situation head-on. It is a calm conviction about who we are and our ability to deal positively with our current situation with success. Why not begin today? Begin by asking yourself the following three questions:

Have I got my health this morning that I can get out of bed and live?

What can I do to help others less well off today?

What am I most grateful for in my life?

Those few queries to yourself will help you realise there is more reason to be optimistic than you previously considered.

Why not begin today to become more aware of your blessings? Instead of remaining in a negative mindset, why not change the mindset to living with joy and positivity?

> *"Always be a first-rate version of yourself, instead of a second-rate version of somebody else."*
> — **Judy Garland**

Socio-economic shifts have been known to affect health. For precisely this reason it is imperative on each one of us to look after our thought processes, thus looking after our health. We should celebrate the good things which are very often the simple things we have in our lives.

4.3   Three Tips towards Conquering that Fear

Fear can be turned into positive energy by choosing to do so. Even if everything around you changes, cast aside your doubts and insecurities and control your situation by taking charge of where you are at:

Be proud of who you are and all of your past achievements.

Be confident in your ability to cope with whatever life *throws* at you.

Be strong in your beliefs.

Although it may seem easier to react negatively, you'll enjoy more lasting benefits if you challenge yourself to find the positive aspects and opportunities that lie within every situation. If you are not in control, you will be *swayed* in every direction, like *a ship without a rudder*. On the other hand, when you are in control, you will be in *"the driving seat of your life"*. You are the only person who can decide how change can be used to your advantage.

I coached somebody who had unexpectedly lost his job and initially considered his situation hopeless and negative. We began by exploring his options and viewed his hobby of playing music at week-ends. We set about designing the development of a music business as a means of income. Three years later he is successful in the music business.

This person took control of his situation and decided to change his mindset from the shock of negativity to positive change.

When you remain in control of your situation and work with somebody who will support you, you will be sure to gain positive results.

Confidence Issues

What would it mean to you to be more confident?

In what areas of your life would you like to be more confident and why?

What or who knocks your confidence?

4.4   Mindfulness

You can only breathe in the NOW. You cannot breathe in the past and you cannot breathe in the future. If only we could learn this truth. How much of our *headspace* is taken up by delving back into our past or going too far forward into the future? Clients often ask me 'how is it possible to be happy as we try to survive these economic challenges?' The answer may be found, in part, by looking at people who have been dealt a seemingly *impossible card* in life and still manage to remain upbeat. How can this be, you may ask?

Try factoring in ten minutes once a week to record at least three positive experiences from your week and continue to do this for six weeks. Through this simple exercise of positive awareness you will find an increasing level of contentment. You will be mindful of and begin to value the positive aspects in your life. This does not mean material possessions, it generally means what we often take for granted: good health, family and friends, a kind act for a neighbour or just a friendly hello. So let's begin today to live every day mindfully. Be grateful for the good things and this awareness will help us deal with the challenges we encounter in our daily lives.

4.5   Mood Watching

Rain, recession, fear of job loss – how do we keep ourselves in a positive mind frame? Coping strategies can include distracting ourselves from our stresses or 'changing the channel'. Do not choose the company of people who only see what's wrong with the world, it will only drag you down. There are good things in everybody's life, but you sometimes have to remember to focus on those same things, or else add them to the mix of your day!

It has been proven that children who are taught optimism and resourcefulness in their early years will have a higher level of contentment down the line. We must all empower ourselves with coping mechanisms for challenging times. Once you realise that you have the power to change yourself rather than waiting for change to come from the outside.

Testimonial 1

Can you imagine living two lives? I can, as this is how I would have described my life before I commenced Life Coaching.

I was living a successful, confident, professional life but a much less successful and less confident private life. Even within my professional life, I always felt my achievements were never enough and I would have described myself as a very negative person.

When I met Nuala she helped me see it was the same person living both lives and she enabled me to see and acknowledge my achievements. She encouraged me to log those achievements and all positivity in my life daily. Recording these positive achievements have helped me experience my professional life and my private life as the 'same person' for the first time in 20 years, that is an amazing feeling!

I now have a much more positive outlook on my overall life and am gaining more confidence in my private life every day.

Thank you Nuala for showing me the way to my new thinking.

Michael, I.T. Management Specialist, Belfast.

Testimonial 2

As the recession hit I was going through a very tough time and when I read one of Nuala's life coaching articles I decided to make an appointment as I felt my life was falling apart.

My father had just died. The Economic Crash left me with no work as I had been employed as a Painter and Decorator. I was just into the third year of a thirty-year large mortgage which I was no longer able to service. Together with all of this my health had deteriorated.

40

At our first meeting, Nuala made me feel very much at ease and comfortable as she made it very clear that anything we discussed would be completely private and confidential. This gave me great trust in Nuala and as a result I could be more open and honest, hence getting the best out of our sessions which would last an hour to an hour and a half. We met for seven sessions in total and they gave me a great foundation to move on with my life with a very positive attitude. Furthermore, Nuala could see my capabilities and she continually stressed and focused on the positives in my life. I had not been able to see those positives myself as I was blinded by so much stress.

She encouraged me to write down what I wanted to achieve in the future and to put a time on it. Also, to write the steps either big or small which needed to be taken to achieve these goals on a daily basis. Nuala also made it clear that it's not about thinking positively and hoping that things will magically happen, but with concrete well planned steps things become achievable with focus and hard work.

With Nuala's coaching I began to "pick myself off the floor" and put a plan together. I began to face my fears and started to live again. The tools that I learned will stay with me for the rest of my life.

Some of the goals Nuala helped me work on and achieve were, improving my diet and I now do at least 5-6 hours of exercise a week. As I faced the fear of the bank I am in talks with them for a debt reduction which is leaving me with a workable payment plan. I looked at changing my career and I undertook a Foundation Course with a view to gaining entry to University. Return to college was hard work and a lot of study but I passed with an average of 68% which did wonders for my self-esteem. Furthermore, I got accepted to one of the top Universities in the country for a Degree course.

All this was achieved in a few short years with Nuala's support.

Thomas, Co. Donegal.

PART 5

Discipline, Habits and the Worry Pattern

5.1   How to Avoid Putting Things off for Another Day

Nothing gets done when it's meant to be done, at best everything is left to the very last minute. We all know the feeling! Procrastinators are not generally the happiest of people though. Putting things off can create tension and lead to havoc in both one's personal and professional life.

Why procrastinate when you know that this is the result?

A fear of the outcome is often enough to stop a person from getting started.

A fear of what people might think. Fear of making a fool of yourself might be holding you back.

A lack of trust in your own ability may also be evident, if you were to dig a little deeper into the depths of your own mind.

A lack of confidence may lie beneath many situations where motivation is lacking. Over time however, procrastination can become so habitual that you are almost unaware of why this frustrating habit has become a part of your natural and instinctive behavioural tendencies. To stop procrastinating, therefore, it is necessary to access that part of your mind where habits are stored.

5.2   Conquer Your Challenges Today

Believing that often the only thing preventing us from reaching our goals is ourselves.

When we continue to do as we've always done we will continue to get the same results. Ireland's 32 Marathon Man, Gerry Duffy has a saying which he repeats often "a small key opens big doors" which we can interpret as starting with small steps towards achieving major goals.

Success in these times can be classed as going from failure to failure without a loss of enthusiasm. So, get motivated today, take action and build your own moment in life!

"Do what you can, with what you have, wherever you are."
— Theodore Roosevelt

5.3   Habits of Effective People

See your future as bright; if you can see it and believe it, you can have it.
– Henry Ford

You can't progress very far looking out of the rear view mirror of life, instead use your imagination to look ahead.

Living in the Past. – If you don't leave your past in the past, it will destroy your future. Live for what today has to offer, not for what yesterday has taken away. Life is a journey that is only travelled once. Today's moments quickly become tomorrow's memories. So appreciate every moment for what it is, because the greatest gift of life is life itself.

Do Not Allow Small Problems Overwhelm You. – Everything is going to be alright, maybe not today but eventually. When you're upset, ask yourself, *"Will this matter to me in a year's time?"* Most of the time it won't. Remember, sometimes bad things in life open up our eyes to the good things we were not previously paying attention to.

Schedule Your Priorities
The key is not to prioritise what's on your schedule, but to schedule your priorities. If it's important, it must be scheduled. What you don't schedule won't get done. Know your priorities and centre your day on those activities.

Never Forget the Main Thing
Never lose sight of the *"big picture,"* keeping the main thing as main thing. Broken focus is the number one reason people fail to get things done. It is not enough to start off on the right track, you must avoid the unnecessary distractions which aim to side-track you.

5.4   Dealing with the Worry Pattern

You do not need to be a victim of worry. Worry is simply an unhealthy and destructive mental habit. Worry has often been described as negative goal setting. You were not born with the worry habit. You acquired it. Because you can change a habit and an acquired attitude, you can also cast worry from your mind. There is a right time to begin an effective attack on your worry habit and that time is NOW. Begin to break that worry pattern at once.

Why, you may ask should we take the worry problem so seriously? The reason is because anxiety is proving to be one of the greatest modern plagues. A well-known psychologist recently stated that there is an '*epidemic*' of fear and worry around. Worry is known to be one of the most destructive of all human diseases, thousands of people today are ill because of this anxiety and worry. Anxieties have a habit of '*turning inwards*' on the personality, causing many forms of ill-health.

It has become an almost iconic sign of our times – the dreaded *stress* word, yet it is still an epidemic that nobody seems to know that much about. Many people appear to be suffering from it, yet nobody knows exactly what causes it, or why. There is as yet no magic pill that we can pop to make it go away. The general consensus, however, is that it is our body's reaction to the demands put on it. Stress seems to affect everyone in different ways – from tension headaches to outbreaks of the common cold. So, what can we do about it? This is where I introduce some ideas that will help you to help yourself in those times of stress.

> "*Life is 10% what happens to me and 90% how I react to it.*"
> – **Lou Holtz**

The first step to take is simply to BELIEVE you can. *Whatever you believe, you can achieve*. Practice emptying the mind of your anxieties each night before retiring. This process is important in overcoming worry because fear thoughts, unless discarded will *clog* the mind/subconscious whilst asleep. However, it is not enough to empty the mind, for the mind cannot function in a vacuum. Therefore, practice replacing those worries with thoughts of faith, hope and peace. Faith will always help overcome anxieties. Cram your mind full of '*I believe*' mantras and you will have no mental room left to accommodate thoughts of worry.

Watch out for the number of '*worry words*' you use in your conversations daily and work on eliminating them.

We waste a lot of our time and energy by worrying. We generally worry about 90% of things which never happen. If we want to beat the worry pattern we should tackle it by taking three essential steps:

- Analyse the situation fearlessly and honestly.

- Figure out the worst case scenario and accept this possibility. Then devote your time and energy towards improving the situation.

- You can always create solutions by rationalising your current situation. Confront that challenge as soon as possible. Do not procrastinate. Just try and shut down the side of the brain that thinks negatively.

5.5   How To Change Perspective on Those Problems

If you've got a problem, don't add to it. Don't make your problem worse by aggravating it with self-pity, anger, or lack of positive faith in the future. The normal reaction is feeling threatened by the problem. Threatened people can become angry people. These are not positive reactions. They will not help solve anything.

Unemployed? Don't hate your company for laying you off. Likewise, don't hate your country for not coming through with a job offer for you. Don't fix the blame, fix the problem. You begin fixing the problem when you begin to control your negative emotions and begin to take action.

Understand that the issue you are facing has been faced by millions of people before. You have untapped potential for dealing with any current challenge, once you are prepared to use that potential. Your reaction to the problem will determine the outcome. You choose your reaction.

I have never met anyone who wanted to swap their problem for someone else's! When you have a difficulty, put it in its proper perspective. The seriousness of it will pass. Ask yourself these questions:

What really is this difficulty?

What is the worst outcome I can get and how will I handle this outcome?

Do I know anybody who has faced a similar problem before and how did he/she overcome it?

How have I managed previous difficulties before?

Is my problem coping with retirement?

Is it lack of money to meet my needs, or is it boredom in my job?

If you think your problem is financial, think again, consider how you have been managing what you have. You probably need to *pare down* some of the expenses that you have taken for granted in the past.

Testimonial 1

When my marriage broke up I was completely torn up. I was searching everywhere for help. Finally, I realised that I had enough knowledge but somehow I could not hang it all together. I needed someone independent but professional, to whom I could refer when I wasn't clear as to where to go or what to do next. On coming across a business card stating, "Live the life you imagined", and the words, "Empowers you for Life", I decided this could be my next move and contacted Nuala. We met, and I have made great progress since. Nuala encouraged me to go on into life especially into socialising, the dimension I was missing and to keep a record of all the good things and successes from each day. She kept in contact with me for about 3 months and, with Nuala as my 'supporter', I managed to walk away from my personal island over the stepping stones to the solid ground of life.

From Mark a separated father

Testimonial 2

The quality of Nuala's coaching was personalised and tailored to my needs. She was always prepared to go that extra mile to meet me where I was at. Nuala proved that she cares greatly about her client's needs. She helped me to believe in myself and my ability to work for myself and I found each session truly inspiring, energising and worthwhile.

She still gives me great encouragement and helps me focus on what I want to do from here, in order to reach my destination. Some of the tools and thoughts Nuala gave me have made an amazing difference to my thinking and actions and I am holding onto those. I have remained really focused and made huge progress on this goal for my new business going forward.

Maura, Web Designer, Dublin

PART 6

Redundancy and Doing it For Yourself

6.1 Dealing with Redundancy, or Too Many Hours

Probably one of the greatest challenges for us is the prospect of doing nothing. Most people have a need to feel productive. The key to dealing with lots of free time is to maximise the use of it.

Looking For Work

Be focused on how you go about looking for a job. Do not do a *blitz*, instead target jobs suitable for your skill base. Consider how you can up-skill, or adapt the skills you already have. Give yourself a specified, regular and limited amount of time each day to job hunt. Do not do it on an *ad-hoc* basis.

Time to Contribute

Do something for others. This will be of benefit to both yourself and the recipient. By helping somebody else it will give you less time for focusing on your own issues and improve your self-esteem. Doing some volunteer work gives you a chance to interact with others from varied backgrounds. What if each one of us made the choice to contribute or volunteer in some small way, be it befriending an isolated elderly person in your area or becoming part of your Tidy Town Committee? Imagine the great benefits for both yourself and the recipient from such contribution.

Check out **www.volunteerireland.ie** to discover a centre near you.

One of our greatest strengths has always been found in our community spirit. This has been particularly evident over the past few years when volunteerism in Ireland has increased ten-fold, proving that community spirit thrives in challenging times.

Take this time to learn or master a skill.

Whether you want to master a language or learn accounting, this is free time which you can spend developing yourself to the maximum. Often, when people are left to their own devices, they find their minds wandering onto negative

53

thoughts and worries. Keep your mind *on track* and occupy it with plenty of things to do. This will also make it easier for you when you do return to a busy lifestyle.

6.2 The Work We Were Born To Do

Finding Your Passion!

What Do You Love Doing?

What Are You Passionate About?

What Do You Really Want?

What Do You Do?

It seems as though every conversation with a new acquaintance gets to this question sooner or later. Whether you work at home or in an office, whether you bring in no income for your daily efforts or can boast of a five-figure salary, the topic of '*what you do*?' is inescapable in our culture.

Less important than what we actually do for a living is our willingness to access who we really are and bring that to our work. As well as our personality, we are spiritual beings – each blest with talents, gifts and resources.

Ours is a '*doing*' culture. We identify ourselves by our accomplishments and how much we can *squeeze* into each day. We need to consider how we can improve at defining ourselves by **WHO** we are, rather than by what we do. This shift from getting our identity from **What We Do**, to getting it from **Who We Are** is a big step towards unfolding of the life we truly desire. Review *The Wheel of Life* (Part 2.4) above in order to explore in more detail WHO you are rather than regarding your employment as your identity.

Seizing That Opportunity

These days, instead of being discouraged by the state of the economy, more and more of us are starting to look within ourselves and become more resourceful in order to earn our *daily bread*. Irish people are now tapping into their creativity with single-minded determination. Approximately 10% of the workforce is currently self-employed. Many home-based businesses make a good starting point for many likely entrepreneurs. We must diversify to survive. See an opportunity and seize that opportunity.

> *"It is never too late to become what you might have been."*
> – **George Elliot**

6.3   ENTREPRENEURSHIP

Where To Begin
Firstly, **DO** something. Don't say, *'I can't'*, however fearful you may feel. Action will empower you. That first step will be the most difficult, but also the most empowering. Keep taking action steps daily. For example up-skill or re-train as soon as possible.

To Do What?
Make a list of your top five *'outside work'* interest areas, remembering where you are most creative. Now explore all job and self-employment possibilities within those areas. Don't even consider, *'I could not do that'*. View this list and decide what re-training is needed? **Just do it**. It will never be a waste of time when it's an area that you're passionate about. Decide now, that you're not going to become part of the *'moaning and whining'* club! Move on and tell people what your definite next step is going to be. This is a new positive message you are sending out.

Do What You Love to Do as Far as Possible
You are designed in such a way that you will be most successful doing the very things that you have the ability to be the very best at. Successful, happy people are invariably those who have taken the time to identify what they do well and most enjoy. Believe in yourself and you will succeed. What you do today will help decide your future.

6.4   Leverage Your Special Talents

It's worth repeating – You are designed in such a way that you will most enjoy doing the very things that you have the ability to be the very best at. Take stock of your unique talents and abilities on a regular basis.

What is it that you do especially well? The very fact that you enjoy this particular work means that you have the capability to be excellent in this area?

What do you do easily and well that is difficult for other people?

Look at that many tasks and responsibilities you have had in the past. What has been most responsible for your success in life and work to date? What has got you the most compliments from other people or past employers?

What do you do that affects the work and performance of other people positively?

One of your great responsibilities in life is to decide for yourself what it is that you really love to do, and then to throw your whole heart into doing that especially well.

You should always focus your best energies and abilities on starting and completing those key tasks where your unique talents enable you to do well and make a significant contribution. The thing you most resist can often be a pointer towards your best living. For example, having to get up and make a speech or to deliver some training can be the most scary experience you might experience, but once you push yourself past that barrier, you will experience a great sense of empowerment.

"Feed your Inspiration and Starve Your Resistance."
– Nick Williams

You cannot do everything but you can do those things in which you excel and where you will make a big difference. This is the key to unlocking your personal potential.

Testimonial 1

Having been let go from my job I wasn't sure what direction to go. All I had were negative thoughts and emotions I found it difficult at the beginning of my first coaching session to fully understand how Life Coaching would really help me. I needn't have been so worried! The sessions with Nuala taught me how a simple goal, backed up with confidence and positivity can overcome so much. Simple baby steps lead to big things being accomplished.

Every night I wrote a few simple lines on what I had achieved that day. This, I felt was a great boost for my self-confidence and made me stronger again. I found on the bad days that re-reading what I wrote kept me aware of where I was and where I wanted to go. I also logged what I wanted to do and the steps I needed to take to fulfil my goals.

I found the sessions benefited me greatly. A lot of the coaching seemed common sense, but when your whole train of thought is negative, the common sense goes out the window. What I learnt from Nuala did not only apply to the one bad situation but really it applies to all the daily challenges and decisions that I encounter throughout my life.

Following our sessions, I was back to my healthy happy self and felt I had made huge progress. At the start, I thought there was no way I could turn my situation around, but as I read once, 'out of no way, a way can be made' and I really felt I came on leaps and bounds thanks to Nuala's help and advice.

Following my experience of being coached by Nuala, I would certainly recommend her to anybody who feels they are drifting along without focus or intention. Nuala holds you accountable from one session to the next, which I found to be a great 'push' for me to act and move on the action steps we agreed on at each session.

Lorna, Office Manager, Co. Kildare.

Testimonial 2

On losing my job in January 2009, when I was not seeing much hope for the future, I found my meeting with Nuala and additional conversations a great help in giving me the confidence and determination to start out building a music career for myself.

Since then I've gone from having an empty diary to doing 3-4 gigs per week, made up of pubs, parties and weddings. I've also upgraded my P.A. system and added lights to cater for the bigger gigs!

I'm currently getting ready to audition for Ireland's Got Talent competition, so here's hoping...

So thanks again Nuala for all your help and giving me the encouragement I needed at the time of our meeting.

Cormac, Freelance Musician, Co. Westmeath.

PART 7

TIME MANAGEMENT,

Workplace Stresses

and Life Balance

7.1   Time Management

Five Tips for General Time Management

Write it down. Whatever you have to do, write it down. We carry far too much around in our heads. This causes undue stress and *burnout* because we are desperately trying to remember everything. Writing it down allows you to get it out of your head, resulting in more "*head space*" for other matters. It also makes things clearer and easier to prioritise as they are recorded in front of you.

Record how long it takes you to do everyday tasks. We often misjudge how long it takes to do our everyday tasks. This leads to poor planning and organisational problems. Become more aware of how long your daily jobs take and you will find yourself able to arrange your day more productively.

Prioritise. List all of your activities and the jobs you need to do and categorise them in order of importance. Many of us spend far too much time on activities which are not of prime importance in our lives. According to Pareto's Principle, 20% of the work we do will account for 80% of the results. Why not spend more time on that 20%?

Say No. Many people find themselves over-burdened because they do not know how to say No to other people's demands on their time.

Check your e-mails in batches. One of the biggest time wasters we encounter is the number of people addicted to checking their e-mails and browsing of the web. This wastes a massive amount of time as it distracts us from the tasks on hand. The key is to decide on a specific time daily to check your e-mails and do it all in one go rather than continuously checking in. This will ensure you work smarter not harder.

Consequences of Not Having a Plan

You feel overwhelmed with too much to do and too little time.

As you struggle to catch up, new tasks and responsibilities just keep rolling in, like the waves of the ocean.

Accept that you will never get on top of ALL your tasks, you can only get control of your time and your life by changing the way you think and work. You will get control of your time when you stop doing less important activities and begin to spend more time on the more important things which make a real difference.

Work/Life Balance

Why Work on Balancing Your Time?
Task Completion gives you:

A positive feeling.

Makes you a happier human being.

You will feel more like a winner.

You will have more energy, enthusiasm and self-esteem.

The more important the completed task, the happier, more confident and empowered you will feel.

7.2   Stress and Sleep Deprivation

Continuous exposure to stress is likely to lead to ill health. The concept of "*burn-out*" is well documented. Sometimes it can be our thoughts more than life events that prolong the stress in our lives. We must remember that thoughts are merely thoughts and not necessarily truths. Negative thoughts, or *jumping* to false conclusions are all causes of stress. Relaxation is the very best remedy in reducing those stress levels. Time out for yourself and pursuing your favourite activity, be it a walk in the park or a swim. Playing a musical instrument or attending a music session. Scheduling time each day for relaxation is necessary in the management of stress. The more we do the things we enjoy, the better we will feel. Unfortunately, sometimes our hectic schedules don't allow much time for relaxation so we need to be flexible and adapt our relaxation techniques accordingly. (See Part 4.4 on *Mindfulness*).

Nowadays experts are putting special focus on a newly identified sleep disorder called "*semi-somnia*". This recently identified plague has the over-use of technology as its main cause. We have always had stress, but this stress has not always interfered with sleep the way today's technology over-users are affected. In earlier years, you may have had a stressful day, but your mind could process problems overnight and you'd wake up the next day refreshed. Nowadays, the ways we relax: shopping online, tweeting while watching television and checking Facebook and e-mails, means our brains are in a permanent state of alert. When bedtime comes around, this can cause big problems. Research has shown that people exposed to the radiation given out by mobile phones before bedtime take longer to enter the deepest stages of sleep. Then there's the fact that whilst reading online, checking Twitter or Facebook could keep your mind "*whirring*", thus taking much longer to get to sleep. Sleep occurs when the mind processes the information we've taken in throughout the day, but the huge amount of material we now consume online can simply be too much to deal with. Experts say the part of the brain that deals with information processing is relatively small and it just cannot cope with the sheer amount of input it's receiving. Information "*mini-breaks*" every ninety minutes throughout the day are necessary to give your mind some space.

7.3   Stress in the Workplace

In the past, stress was associated with managerial pressures, so called Executive Stress. Many managers remain in the highest risk of stress category resulting in working longer hours on a continual basis simply to '*keep up*'. Occupational stress during the Celtic Tiger Era was largely self-induced as 'Celtic Cubs' were *chasing the dream*, driven by the desire to make their fortune, fast car, few foreign holidays annually and more than one home. Now however, things are changing fast as organisations are making staff redundant and contracting part-time workers. The stress factors have changed. The stresses now emanate more from the lack of employment or part-time work, financial pressures and too much free time.

A combination of *'work over-load'* and *'quality under load'* are common causes for stress. Workers involved in repetitive tasks, working under close measurement and supervision are likely to be stressed, particularly if their training, equipment and/or opportunity for breaks are inadequate. Here, it is necessary to determine what is unacceptable. Giving all of yourself is not the answer, it simply leaves you drained. On the other hand, when you assert your boundaries you maintain your self-esteem and, as a result, you have a more worthwhile contribution to give to your work.

When companies want to create positive work environments, they are happy to invest in Life Coaching for their **most important customers, their employees.** The return on such investment will come in the form of:

Higher levels of employee motivation.

Increased creativity, productivity, and commitment that will help move the organization forward.

They will realise that every employee is a unique human being, not just a *cog in a machine*, and each employee is involved in helping the company meet its goals. Then every individual's input is valued by management.

An employer's legal duty of care towards his/her staff should necessitate a Plan of Action, which can be undertaken based on stress assessments in the work place:-

Redesign of work to expand the area of control and responsibility of each individual.

The elimination of monotonous or paced work.

Improved and on-going training to promote new opportunities for learning and promotion.

Improved design of work station layout and a reduction of noise levels. Regulation of incorrect temperatures and enhancement of natural light.

Employers are slowly *waking up* to the fact that a healthy stress-free workplace simply makes sound business sense. A happy work/life balance for each employee is essential, not just for personal contentment and a healthy work environment but also leads to better work results.

7.4   Regain Control of Your Life and Visualisation

These days every news channel is forecasting '*doom and gloom*'. You can manage to '*switch out*' by realising that when things seem hopeless there is always a chance for optimism and opportunity. When situations seem impossible things become possible. What makes some people keep on going when others would have given up? What do they see that the rest of us do not?

The answer is, that these people have a vision, they really can see the end result of what they want to achieve. They can see it, hear it, feel it, they can image their success. Not only that, they have the ability to hold that focus, to keep that vision clear in their mind, no matter what set-backs may occur. This ability to imagine and visualise their success also creates a clear expectancy that they will win, whatever winning means to them.

> *"Whatever the mind can conceive and believe*
> *it can achieve."*
> – **Napoleon Hill**

If you were to act in every way as if you knew you were going to win, or knew that you were going to succeed, can you imagine the increase in confidence and positive energy you would experience? Imagine what it might feel like if you had twice as much energy and twice as much enthusiasm as you currently have.

How much easier would problem solving be?

How much easier would it be to push past limits or barriers and be open to all possibilities?

Top sports people know that you have to "*keep your eye on the ball*", to keep your focus, and to keep on going. The ability to visualise is essential. Commit, focus, believe and achieve. Your thoughts and the mental images which you create in turn create emotional energy which directs your actions. The more vivid your visualisations and the more confident your thoughts, together, create more positive energy to drive your actions.

7.5 How are You Dealing with Apparent Failures?

Permission to fail is permission to try. Failure may be seen as deferred achievement. Fear of failure inhibits risk of any sort. It is vital to realise rejections are *par for the course* and they are simply only one person's opinion. So if your boss says "*you're superfluous to requirements*", what you hear is that "*you're useless and you're not needed*". This is only your interpretation of events because it's not what happens in your life that matters, it's how you interpret and deal with what happens.

There is only one way to Fail and that is to Quit. When faced with an apparent defeat you can either get angry or pretend it never happened and everything is fine. You can make excuses about what happened, or blame other people for the experience. These are all the ways you don't want to respond.

When you get angry you're giving up control of yourself to someone or something else. You can't control other people, you can only control yourself. It is necessary to recognise that **you, and only you, are responsible for every experience you have**. So, if you didn't have the experience you wanted, look to yourself to figure out **why and what** you can do to obtain a different experience next time.

You have to view every **apparent failure** as a **learning opportunity** and make the appropriate changes. You will have to accept full and total responsibility for what happened, choose the next appropriate action and determine to follow through on that action.

Know that **failure is merely feedback** and learn from it. Look at it in a non-emotional way and ask yourself those three simple questions:

What worked?

What did not work?

What must I do differently in the future?

Failure is not an accident. It is there to teach you something. It tells you what to do more of and what to do less of. Look at how things came about this way. Decide what you need to do to adjust the situation and what to do next. Develop a tolerance for mistakes and failures, these are your most powerful teachers. In fact, those who have never experienced failure have missed out on valued learning experiences. It's not **how you fall**, it's **how you pick yourself up** that matters. Celebrate the fact that the road to success is *paved* with many apparent failures. Decide today how you are going to handle them.

Success can be classed as going from failure to failure without a loss of enthusiasm. We cannot always control what happens to us, but we can control how we respond.

Testimonial 1

I am 38 years of age and have been working in a job for the last 3 years and have been very 'Brain Dead'.

Our starting point when I met with Nuala was to look at areas whereby I would be a happier and more fulfilled individual. Having applied for an alternative job, Nuala and myself designed a Plan B if original plan does not work out. She worked with me so that I would focus less on one area in order to develop the many aspects of my life using the Wheel of Life *tool. She encouraged me to be more prepared and positively focused if next job does not work out.*

By using my hobby this could quite possibly turn into a successful business. I am already working on this route. I have changed my lateral thinking to a broader version and feel that the possibilities are endless.

Life coaching has also got me working on daily goals for myself and I am already rising an hour earlier daily in order to get ahead!

3 out of 4 tasks on my list today completed and flying it!

Connie, Co. Roscommon

Testimonial 2

I felt lucky to have met Nuala on a business course we both attended. I had recently lost my job and was in the process of setting up a small business, but I wasn't sure if this was the way for me to go.

Having spoken with Nuala, I realised a few things about myself and my future. As time went on I opened my mind up to opportunities that were out there.

The business which I was in the process of setting up is going very well due to my new attitude towards it. I now have another project underway which has excellent potential.

Thank you Nuala for the great inspiration and help.

Noel, Driving Instructor, Co. Leitrim.

PART 8

Customer Care

8.1 Looking After Your Customer

How often have we stood exasperated in a queue only to find, when reaching the end of that queue, not a greeting, a smile or a gesture of any sort? I'm referring to the many times when either in a doctor's surgery, a chain store or petrol station that we, as customers, have not been acknowledged as a human presence.

Have you ever had the experience of staff deciding that their interaction with a fellow staff member supersedes their need to greet you, the customer in front of them?

Have you ever encountered the receptionist, either in a legal office, an optician's or dentist's, who is so busy texting or typing behind their desk, that you get the feeling that you are an inconvenience.

Is it not well time then that we all try to 're-ignite' that name that has spread around the world as the *friendly Irish*.

When you have customers, you must have customer service. Everybody talks about the importance of good customer service, but not all businesses seem to follow through with it. Good customer service is no longer enough. It has to be a superior service. In a nutshell, it means doing:

What you say you will

When you say you will

How you say you will and

At the price you promised

plus

A little extra tossed in to say '*I appreciate your business.*'

Customers who are delighted and truly amazed by your service, will not only remain loyal, they will also be an excellent source of referral for you.

Engage with your customers. Do not wait for them to have to voice their concerns. Regular and proactive communication around product and service satisfaction will identify any problems before they get out of hand. Customer feedback will also help your company to measure satisfaction and identify areas for improvement.

Just as you have financial and sales processes in place, is it not equally or even more important to have a sound customer service process? It's all about customer satisfaction. Just meeting the needs of your customers doesn't *hack it* any more. Always go that extra mile for your customer.

> *"There are no traffic jams when travelling that extra mile."*
> – **Roger Staubach**

8.2   Why is Good Customer Service Vital?

Great customer service can be recognised in how your business is able to constantly and consistently exceed the needs of the customer. Let us begin by querying WHY great customer service is vital today? Great customer service adds value and customers are turning their backs on businesses who do not deliver this value. There's no way around it. No shortcuts. Customers demand value for their money now more than ever. If they do not receive that value, *they are out that door.* Before you know it, you're out of business.

A research company recently discovered that the average business never hears from 96% of its unhappy customers. **It costs five times more to attract a new client.** If the customer feels badly about how they have been treated, they will tell their friends and family about the experience. On the other hand, an unhappy customer whose complaint was satisfactorily resolved, will tell up to five people about the positive treatment they received.

8.3   It all Comes Down to Performance.

The business that always pushes to do better will have the best results. All successful businesses reinforce the same lesson. In order to stand out from the crowd and get people's attention, you must strive to **OUT-PERFORM** every time. Being just 0.03% better is not enough. Your customers deserve much more.

Scrutinise all aspects of your business. Make a massive difference wherever and whenever you can. Create that competitive edge which will leave a lasting positive memory. Yes, it's hard work, but your customers deserve it and going that extra mile quickly differentiates you from the rest.

Today, performance is more important than ever. Social media gives customers the opportunity to inform the world which companies are performing, and which ones are not. And their observations, positive or negative, will spread like *wildfire*. This new reality is nothing to fear, it offers your business a great opportunity to stand out. Never before were the voices of customers heard so clearly. Check out Trip Advisor as just one example of direct opinions. Also, Twitter and Facebook.

8.4   Make that Difference and Out-Perform Every Time.

Every organization, small or large, can set their own high standards and create policies around how their customers are treated:

How quickly are your customers dealt with when they walk into your reception area or phone for your service?

How soon are telephone messages responded to?

What is the acceptable lead-time between a telephone enquiry and the delivery of information requested?

There is always room for improvement. There are many opportunities to help strengthen the customer bond which are not currently being exploited.

Do not delay in providing that superior customer service.

Testimonial

Bill experienced the Economic Crash at its worst during 2007. He endured financial shock. He decided from rock bottom the only way was Up. He turned around his thought processes and set *in train* goals which he urgently needed to reach, on both a physical and psychological level. He undertook weight loss and began a brand new business. He clarified those goals and reached his desired targets within the time he proposed.

"When I met Nuala in July, 2012 I had come a long way from the crash in 2007 I had read some of her articles and realised from the work I had done solo that I could at this stage benefit from her support and encouragement on the journey I had commenced some years previously. Nuala proved to be that support which I needed to re-focus my goals and set up new Action Steps with a Time-Line.

She began by acknowledging the great progress I had made with my life since 2007. She assured me that I was at a very positive starting point for coaching and she knew that whatever goal I decided on I would work tirelessly until I reached it.

I came to her with a new goal I wanted to work on and we mutually decided on the immediate action steps I should take to set the process in motion. We met fortnightly over a period of 4 sessions.

I have felt increased momentum and drive towards both my personal and business goals since meeting up with Nuala. She has held me accountable and has not allowed me "to slip back or sideways" on my journey. Because I have a very busy mind she has kept me focused on the main goal before moving on to tackle another.

*Since I began my coaching journey I have become so convinced of the great benefits to be gained from the whole process, I have commenced an intensive Coaching Diploma Course myself whereby I will be able to be **that support and encouragement for other people**. This will compliment my*

Motivational Weight Loss programme which has been another one of my aims and I will then be supporting people on their holistic mind/body journey.

Thanks Nuala for giving me the insight to Life Coaching and the great benefits to be gained from same. I have gained in both personal and work life as I continue to re-shape my goals as Director my own business.

Bill, Company Director, Co. Cavan.

IN CONCLUSION

Where Do We Go From Here?

There is magic in believing in our capabilities at the moment, believing in our future potential, believing that we are worthy human beings with a purpose for being alive. However, the chance is present every moment to realise new dreams, to progress to new heights, to switch whatever course we are presently travelling on. We just need to adopt a changed attitude, commitment to a new idea, and the accompanying belief in the idea's potential.

> *"Everybody can be great because anybody can serve their fellow man. You don't have to have a college degree to serve."*
> – **Martin Luther King**

Living in the past

You cannot progress very far looking out of the rear view mirror of life, instead use your imagination to look ahead.

If you don't leave your past in the past, it will destroy your future. Live for what today has to offer, not for what yesterday has taken away. Life is a journey that is only travelled once. Today's moments quickly become tomorrow's memories. So appreciate every moment for what it is, because the **greatest gift of life is life itself**.

How we survive are urgent and important matters right now. We must query ourselves as to what's special about what we have and what we can improve?

We are all products of our cumulative life experiences. It is because of those experiences and choices we have made that have brought us to where we are today. So let us congratulate ourselves on our accomplishments and work in supporting each other. If we all become what we should be we can *"set the world on fire"*. In life you either have a result OR you have an excuse. Choose today which it will be for you.

> *"Take that first step in faith. You don't have to see the whole staircase, just that first step."*
> – **Martin Luther King**

APPENDIX ONE

Book Listing

BOOK LISTING (Some recommended reading)

1. *The Power of Now* – Eckhart Tolle

2. *Take Time for Your Life* – Cheryl Richardson

3. *Smart Work – Guide for Mutual Understanding in the Work Place* – Lucy Freedman

4. *Living Your Best Life* – Laura Berman Fortgang

5. *The Seven Spiritual Habits for Success* – Deepak Chopra

6. *The Four Agreements* – Don Miguel Ruiz

7. *The Miracle of Change* – Dennis Wholey

8. *3 Sides of You – Unlocking the Way you think, work and love* – S. Seich

9. *Reach for the Summit: Definite Dozen System for Succeeding at Whatever You Do* – Pat Summitt (with Sally Jenkins)

10. *The Seven Habits of Highly Effective People* – Stephen R. Covey

11. *Stress at Work* – Mary Hartley

12. *Shortcuts to Keeping your Cool* – Gael Lindenfield.

13. *Unleash the Power Within* – Tony Robbins

14. *Getting Things Done* – Mark Fritz

15. *The Artist's Way* – Julia Cameron

16. *Count Your Blessings* – Dr. John F. Demartini

17. *Yes I Can* – Con Hurley

18. *The Power of Positive Thinking* – Norman Vincent Peale

19. *Never Too Late* – Lowell Sheppard

20. *Think and Grow Rich* – Napoleon Hill

21. *The Breakthrough Experience* – Dr. John F. Demarrtini

22. *Basics Before Buzz* – Kevin Kelly.

APPENDIX TWO

New Year's Resolutions

New Year Reality Check

As another year dawns it's an ideal time to reflect on your achievements, celebrate your wins and consider your goals for the coming year and beyond.

December is a good time to think about fresh starts. We all need a fresh start now and then, and the beginning of a new year is an ideal time to begin. We have endured some complex years recently. Many of us enter the New Year with lowered expectations. But there will be opportunities too. There is fear though, that our *economy* is going to make earning a decent living more tricky. Fear causes worry. It gradually *digs itself in* until it paralyses our reasoning and it can *kill* our initiative. During an economic downturn we can be filled with fear and worry and both of those states of mind can be really destructive. So why not instead choose the coming year to be:

Another year, another chance
To start our lives anew
This time we'll leap old barriers
To have a real breakthrough.
We'll take one little step
And then we'll take one more,
Our unlimited potential
We'll totally explore.

For the New Year let us:

Get rid of non-essential numbers. These include, age and weight. Let the doctor worry about them. That is why you pay him/her!

Never let the brain idle. An idle mind is the *devil's workshop*. Keep learning. Learn more about the computer, golf, gardening, whatever....

Enjoy the simple things. Laugh often.

Be ALIVE while you are alive. Do not die with the *music still in you.*

Cherish your health. If it is good, preserve it.

If it is unstable, improve it.

If it is beyond what you can improve get help NOW!

Don't take guilt trips. Take a trip to the next county or to a foreign country but NOT to where the guilt is!

Keep cheerful friends. Negative people bring you down and surround you with their negativity, so why allow that to happen?

END

NOTES

NOTES